Psalms

D0707211

Psalms

The Prayer Book of the Bible

Dietrich Bonhoeffer

Augsburg
MINNEAPOLIS

PSALMS
The Prayer Book of the Bible

This volume is a translation of *Das Gebetbuch der Bibel*, 8th edition, published in 1966 by Verlag für Missionsund Bibel-Kunde, Bad Salzuflen, Germany.

Large-quantity purchases or custom editions of this book are available at a discount from the publisher. For more information, contact the sales department at Augsburg Fortress, Publishers, 1-800-328-4648, or write to: Sales Director, Augsburg Fortress, Publishers, P.O. Box 1209, Minneapolis, MN 55440-1209.

Scripture passages are from the Revised Standard Version of the Bible, copyright © 1946, 1952, 1971, 1989 by the Division of Christian Education of the National Council of the Churches of Christ in the USA. Used by permission.

Cover design by Michelle L. N. Cook

ISBN 0-8066-1439-0

The paper used in this publication meets the minimum requirements of American National Standard for Information Sciences— Permanence of Paper for Printed Library Materials, ANSI Z329.48-1984. ♾ ™

Manufactured in the U.S.A.   AF 9-1439

Contents

7

"Lord, Teach Us to Pray!"

So spoke the disciples to Jesus. In making this request, they confessed that they were not able to pray on their own, that they had to learn to pray. The phrase "learning to pray" sounds strange to us. If the heart does not overflow and begin to pray by itself, we say, it will never "learn" to pray. But it is a dangerous error, surely very widespread among Christians, to think that the heart can pray by itself. For then we confuse wishes, hopes, sighs, laments, rejoicings—all of which the heart can do by itself—with prayer. And we confuse earth and heaven, man and God. Prayer does not mean simply to pour out one's heart. It means rather to find the way

9

to God and to speak with him, whether the heart
is full or empty. No man can do that by himself.
For that he needs Jesus Christ.

The disciples want to pray, but they do not
know how to do it. That can be very painful, to
want to speak with God and not to be able to,
to have to be speechless before God, to discover
that every call to him dies within itself, that
heart and mouth speak an absurd language
which God does not want to hear. In this need we
seek out men who are able to help us, who know
something about prayer. If one among us who
is able to pray would only take the other along
in his prayer, if we could pray along with him,
then we could be helped! Certainly experienced
Christians can help us in this way a great deal.
But they can do it only through him who must
himself help them, and to whom they direct us
if they are true teachers in prayer, namely
through Jesus Christ. If he takes us with him in
his prayer, if we are privileged to pray along
with him, if he lets us accompany him on his
way to God and teaches us to pray, then we are

free from the agony of prayerlessness. But that is precisely what Jesus Christ wants to do. He wants to pray with us and to have us pray with him, so that we may be confident and glad that God hears us. When our will wholeheartedly enters into the prayer of Christ, then we pray correctly. Only in Jesus Christ are we able to pray, and with him we also know that we shall be heard.

And so we must learn to pray. The child learns to speak because his father speaks to him. He learns the speech of his father. So we learn to speak to God because God has spoken to us and speaks to us. By means of the speech of the Father in heaven his children learn to speak with him. Repeating God's own words after him, we begin to pray to him. We ought to speak to God and he wants to hear us, not in the false and confused speech of our heart, but in the clear and pure speech which God has spoken to us in Jesus Christ.

God's speech in Jesus Christ meets us in the Holy Scriptures. If we wish to pray with confidence and gladness, then the words of Holy Scripture will have to be the solid basis of our prayer. For here we know that Jesus Christ, the Word of God, teaches us to pray. The words which come from God become, then, the steps on which we find our way to God.

Learning to Pray
in the Name of Jesus

Now there is in the Holy Scriptures a book which is distinguished from all other books of the Bible by the fact that it contains only prayers. The book is the Psalms. It is at first very surprising that there is a prayerbook in the Bible. The Holy Scripture is the Word of God to us. But prayers are the words of men. How do prayers then get into the Bible? Let us make no mistake about it, the Bible is the Word of God even in the Psalms. Then are these prayers to God also God's own word? That seems rather difficult to understand. We grasp it only when we remember that we can learn true prayer only from Jesus Christ, from the word of the Son of

God, who lives with us men, to God the Father, who lives in eternity. Jesus Christ has brought every need, every joy, every gratitude, every hope of men before God. In his mouth the word of man becomes the Word of God, and if we pray his prayer with him, the Word of God becomes once again the word of man. All prayers of the Bible are such prayers which we pray together with Jesus Christ, in which he accompanies us, and through which he brings us into the presence of God. Otherwise there are no true prayers, for only in and with Jesus Christ can we truly pray.

If we want to read and to pray the prayers of the Bible and especially the Psalms, therefore, we must not ask first what they have to do with us, but what they have to do with Jesus Christ. We must ask how we can understand the Psalms as God's Word, and then we shall be able to pray them. It does not depend, therefore, on whether the Psalms express adequately that which we feel at a given moment in our heart. If we are to pray aright, perhaps it is quite necessary that we pray contrary to our own heart. Not what we want to pray is important, but what God wants us to pray. If we were dependent entirely on ourselves, we would probably pray only the fourth petition of the Lord's Prayer. But God wants it otherwise. The richness of the Word of God ought to determine our prayer, not the poverty of our heart.

Thus if the Bible also contains a prayerbook, we learn from this that not only that Word which he has to say to us belongs to the Word of God, but also that word which he wants to hear from us, because it is the word of his beloved Son. This is pure grace, that God tells us how we can speak with him and have fellowship with him. We can do it by praying in the name of Jesus Christ. The Psalms are given to us to this end, that we may learn to pray them in the name of Jesus Christ.

In response to the request of the disciples, Jesus gave them the Lord's Prayer. Every prayer is contained in it. Whatever is included in the petitions of the Lord's Prayer is prayed aright; whatever is not included is no prayer. All the

prayers of Holy Scripture are summarized in
the Lord's Prayer, and are contained in its im-
measurable breadth. They are not made superfluous by the Lord's Prayer but constitute the
inexhaustible richness of the Lord's Prayer as
the Lord's Prayer is their summation. Luther
says of the Psalter: "It penetrates the Lord's
Prayer and the Lord's Prayer penetrates it, so
that it is possible to understand one on the basis
of the other and to bring them into joyful harmony." Thus the Lord's Prayer becomes the
touchstone for whether we pray in the name of
Jesus Christ or in our own name. It makes good
sense, then, that the Psalter is often bound together in a single volume with the New Testament. It is the prayer of the Christian church
It belongs to the Lord's Prayer.

Who Prays the Psalms?

Of the 150 Psalms, 73 are attributed to King David, 12 to the songmaster Asaph who was appointed by David, 12 to the Levitical family of the children of Korah working under David, 2 to King Solomon, one to the music masters Heman and Ethan, probably employed by David and Solomon. Thus it is understandable that the name of David has been connected with the Psalter in special ways.

It is reported that after David's secret anointing as king, he was called to play the harp for King Saul, who was abandoned by God and plagued by an evil spirit. "And whenever the evil spirit from God was upon Saul, David took the lyre and played it with his hand; so Saul was refreshed, and was well, and the evil spirit departed from him" (1 Samuel 16:23). That may have been the beginning of the writing of the Psalms by David. In the power of the spirit of God, which had come upon him at the time of his anointing, he drove away the evil spirit through his song. No Psalm has been transmitted to us from the time prior to the anointing. The songs which later were accepted into the canon of the Holy Scriptures were first prayed by the one called to be the messianic king, from whom the promised king Jesus Christ was to descend.

According to the witness of the Bible, David is, as the anointed king of the chosen people of God, a prototype of Jesus Christ. What happens to him happens to him for the sake of the one who is in him and who is said to proceed from him, namely Jesus Christ. And he is not unaware of this, but "being therefore a prophet, and knowing that God had sworn with an oath to him that he would set one of his descendants upon his throne, he foresaw and spoke of the resurrection of the Christ" (Acts 2:30 f.). David was a witness to Christ in his office, in his life, and in his words. The New Testament says even more. In the Psalms of David the promised Christ himself already speaks (Hebrews 2:12; 10:5) or, as may also be indicated, the Holy Spirit (Hebrews 3:7). These same words which David spoke, therefore, the future Messiah spoke through him. The prayers of David were prayed also by Christ. Or better, Christ himself prayed them through his forerunner David.

This short comment on the New Testament sheds significant light on the entire Psalter. It relates the Psalter to Christ. How that is to be understood in detail we still have to consider. But it is important to note that even David did not pray out of the personal exuberance of his heart, but out of the Christ who dwelled in him. To be sure, the one who prays his Psalms remains himself. But in him and through him it is Christ who prays. The last words of old David express the same thing in a hidden way: "The oracle of David, the son of Jesse, the oracle of the man who was raised on high, the anointed of the God of Jacob, the sweet psalmist of Israel: 'The Spirit of the Lord speaks by me, his word is upon my tongue' "; and then follows a final prophecy about the coming king of righteousness, Jesus Christ (2 Samuel 23:1 f.).

Therefore we are once again led to the realization which we affirmed earlier. Certainly not all the Psalms are by David, and there is no word of the New Testament which places the entire Psalter in the mouth of Christ. Nevertheless, the intimations already alluded to must be sufficiently important to us to point to the entire Psalter, which is decisively bound up with the name of David. And Jesus himself says about the Psalms in general that they announced his death and his resurrection and the preaching of the Gospel (Luke 24:44 ff.).

How is it possible for a man and Jesus Christ to pray the Psalter together? It is the incarnate Son of God, who has borne every human weakness in his own flesh, who here pours out the heart of all humanity before God and who stands in our place and prays for us. He has known torment and pain, guilt and death more deeply than we. Therefore it is the prayer of the human nature assumed by him which comes here before God. It is really our prayer, but since he knows us better than we know ourselves and since he himself was true man for our sakes, it is also really his prayer, and it can become our prayer only because it was his prayer.

Who prays the Psalms? David (Solomon, Asaph, etc.) prays, Christ prays, we pray. We—that is, first of all the entire community in which alone the vast richness of the Psalter can be prayed, but also finally every individual insofar as he participates in Christ and his community and prays their prayer. David, Christ, the church, I myself, and wherever we consider all of this together we recognize the wonderful way in which God teaches us to pray.

Names,
Music, Verse Form

The Hebrew title of the Psalms also means "hymns." Psalm 72:20 refers to all preceding Psalms as "the prayers of David." Both items are surprising and yet understandable. To be sure, at first glance, the Psalms contain exclusively neither hymns nor prayers. In spite of that the didactic poems or the songs of lament are also basically hymns, for they serve to glorify God, and even those Psalms which do not contain any address to God (e.g. Psalms 1, 2, 78) may be called prayers, for they serve to submerge in God's will and purpose the one who prays them. The word "Psalter" originally referred to a musical instrument, and was first used only

in a secondary sense as a designation for a col-
lection of prayers which were offered to God in
the form of songs.

The Psalms, as we have them today, are for
the most part set to music for liturgical use. Vo-
cal parts and instruments of all sorts work together. Again it is David to whom the particular
liturgical music is ascribed. As at one time his
harp playing drove away the evil spirit, so the
sacred liturgical music is such an effective power
that occasionally the same word can be used for
it as is used for prophetic preaching (1 Chron-
icles 25:2). Many of the titles of the Psalms
which are difficult to understand are directions
for the musicians. This also applies to the "Sela"
which often occurs in the middle of a Psalm
and which apparently signals an interlude. "The
Sela indicates that one must be still and quickly
think through the words of the Psalm; for they
demand a quiet and restful soul, which can grasp
and hold to that which the Holy Spirit there
presents and offers" (Luther).

The Psalms were probably most often sung

antiphonally. They were particularly well suited for that through the verse form, according to which the two parts of a verse are so connected that they express in different words essentially the same thought. This is called parallelism. This form is not simply accidental. It encourages us not to allow the prayer to be cut off prematurely, and it invites us to pray together with one another. That which seems to be unnecessary repetition to us, who are inclined to pray too hurriedly, is actually proper immersion and concentration in prayer. It is at the same time the sign that many, indeed all believers, pray with different words yet with one and the same word. Therefore the verse form in particular summons us to pray the Psalms together.

Congregational Worship and the Psalms

In many churches the Psalms are read or sung every Sunday, or even daily, in succession. These churches have preserved a priceless treasure, for only with daily use does one appropriate this divine prayerbook. When read only occasionally, these prayers are too overwhelming in design and power and tend to turn us back to more palatable fare. But whoever has begun to pray the Psalter seriously and regularly will soon give a vacation to other little devotional prayers and say: "Ah, there is not the juice, the strength, the passion, the fire which I find in the Psalter. It tastes too cold and too hard" (Luther).

Therefore, wherever we no longer pray the Psalms in our churches, we must take up the

Psalter that much more in our daily morning and evening prayers, reading and praying together at least several Psalms every day so that we succeed in reading through this book a number of times each year, getting into it deeper and deeper. We also ought not to select Psalms at our own discretion, thinking that we know better what we ought to pray than does God himself. To do that is to dishonor the prayerbook of the Bible. In the ancient church it was not unusual to memorize "the entire David." In one of the eastern churches this was a prerequisite for the pastoral office. The church father St. Jerome says that one heard the Psalms being sung in the fields and gardens in his time. The Psalter impregnated the life of early Christianity. Yet more important than all of this is the fact that Jesus died on the cross with the words of the Psalter on his lips.

Whenever the Psalter is abandoned, an incomparable treasure vanishes from the Christian church. With its recovery will come unsuspected power.

Classification

We shall arrange the subjects dealt with in the Psalter prayers in the following manner: the creation; the law; holy history; the Messiah; the church; life; suffering; guilt; enemies; the end. It would not be difficult to arrange these according to the Lord's Prayer and to show how the Psalter is totally absorbed in the prayer of Jesus. But in order not to anticipate this result of our observations, we want to remain with the arrangement inferred from the Psalter itself.

The Creation

The Scripture proclaims God to be the Creator of heaven and earth. Many Psalms summon us to bring him honor, praise, and thanksgiving. There is, however, no single Psalm which speaks only of the creation. It is always the God who has already revealed himself to his people in his word who is said to be known as the Creator of the world. Because God has spoken to us, because God's name has been revealed to us, we can believe in him as the Creator. Otherwise we could not know him. The creation is a picture of the power and the faithfulness of God, which he has demonstrated to us in his revelation in Jesus Christ. We worship the Creator who has revealed himself as the Redeemer.

Psalm 8 praises the name of God and his gracious act to man as the crown of his work. But that is incomprehensible on the basis of the creation alone. Psalm 19 cannot speak of the splendor of the movement of the heavenly bodies without at the same time mentioning in abrupt and unexpected insertions the much greater splendor of the revelation of God's law and the call to repentance. Psalm 29 lets us wonder at the frightful power of God in the thunder, and yet its goal lies in the power, the blessing, and the peace which God sends to his people. Psalm 104 fixes our eyes on the fullness of the work of God, and sees it at the same time as nothing before him whose honor alone remains eternal and who finally must blot out sin.

The creation Psalms are not lyrical poems, but instruction for the people of God in which, coming to know the grace of salvation, they are led to know and to honor the Creator of the world.

The creation serves the believer, and everything created by God is good if received with thanksgiving (1 Timothy 4:3 f.). But we are able to give thanks only for that which stands in harmony with the revelation of God in Jesus Christ. The creation with all its gifts is there for the sake of Jesus Christ. So we thank God for the grandeur of his creation with, in, and through Jesus Christ, to whom we belong.

The Law

The three Psalms (1, 19, 119) which in a special way make the law of God the object of thanks, praise, and petition seek to show us, above all, the blessing of the law. Under "law," then, is to be understood usually the entire salvation act of God and the direction for a new life in obedience. Joy in the law and in the commands of God comes to us if God has given the great new direction to our life through Jesus Christ. That God could at one time conceal his command from me (Psalm 119:19), that he could allow me one day not to recognize his will, is the deepest anxiety of the new life.

It is grace to know God's commands. They re-

lease us from self-made plans and conflicts. They
make our steps certain and our way joyful. God
gives his commands in order that we may fulfill
them, and "his commandments are not burden-
some" (1 John 5:3) for him who has found all
salvation in Jesus Christ. Jesus has himself been
under the law and has fulfilled it in total obedience to the Father. God's will becomes his joy,
his nourishment. So he gives thanks in us for
the grace of the law and grants to us joy in its
fulfillment. Now we confess our love for the law,
we affirm that we gladly keep it, and we ask
that we may continue to be kept blameless in it.
We do that not in our own power, but we pray it
in the name of Jesus Christ who is for us and
in us.

Psalm 119 becomes especially difficult for us,
perhaps, because of its length and monotony. In
this case a rather slow, quiet, patient advance
from word to word, from sentence to sentence, is
helpful. Then we recognize that the apparent
repetitions are always new variations on one
theme, namely the love of God's word. As this

love can never cease, so also the words which confess it can never cease. They want to accompany us through all of life, and they become in their simplicity the prayer of the child, of the young man, and of the old man.

Holy History

Psalms 78, 105, and 106 tell us about the history of the people of God on earth, about the electing grace and faithfulness of God and the unfaithfulness and the ingratitude of his people. Psalm 78 is not addressed as a prayer to anyone. How ought we to pray these Psalms? Psalm 106 summons us to thanksgiving, to praise, to commitment, to petition, to confession of sin, to the call for help in the light of the past history of salvation: thanksgiving for the goodness of God, which continues with respect to his people into eternity, which also we contemporaries experience as did our fathers; praise for the miracles which God works for our benefit, from the redemption of his people out of Egypt all the way to Golgotha; commitment to keep the command of God more faithfully than before; petitions concerning the grace of God according to his promise; confession of our own sins, unfaithfulness, and unworthiness in the face of such compassion; call for help concerning the final gathering and redemption of the people of God.

We pray these Psalms when we regard all that God does once for his people as done for us, when we confess our guilt and God's grace, when we hold God true to his promises on the basis of his former benefits and request their fulfillment, and when we finally see the entire history of God with his people fulfilled in Jesus Christ, through whom we have been helped and will be helped. For the sake of Jesus Christ we bring God thanksgiving, petition, and confession.

The Messiah

God's holy history comes to fulfillment in the sending of the Messiah. According to Jesus' own interpretation, the Psalter has prophesied of this Messiah (Luke 24:44). Psalms 22 and 69 are known to the church as the passion psalms.

Jesus himself prayed the beginning of Psalm 22 on the cross and so clearly made it his prayer. Hebrews 2:12 places verse 22 in the mouth of Christ. Verse 8 and verse 18 are direct predictions of the crucifixion of Jesus. David himself may have once prayed this Psalm in his own song. If so, he did this as the king, anointed by God and therefore persecuted by men, from whom Jesus Christ would descend. He did it as the one who bore Christ in himself. But Christ himself used this prayer and for the first time gave it its full meaning. We can thus pray this Psalm only in the fellowship of Jesus Christ, as those who have participated in the suffering of Christ. We pray this Psalm, not on the basis of our fortuitous personal suffering, but on the basis of the suffering of Christ which has also come upon us. But we always hear Jesus Christ pray with us, and through him that Old Testament king; and repeating this prayer without being able to experience it or consider it in its deepest sense, we nevertheless walk with the praying Christ before the throne of God.

In Psalm 69, verse 5 tends to cause difficulty because here Christ complains to God about his foolishness and guilt. Certainly David spoke here of his personal guilt. But Christ speaks of the guilt of all men, also about the guilt of David and my own guilt which he has taken upon himself, and borne, and for which he now suffers the wrath of the Father. The true man Jesus Christ prays in this Psalm and includes us in his prayer.

Psalms 2 and 110 witness to the victory of
Christ over his enemies, the establishment of his
kingdom, and worship by the people of God.
Even here the prophecy makes a contact with
David and with his kingdom. But we already
recognize in David the coming Christ. Luther
calls Psalm 110 "the truly supreme chief Psalm
of our dear Lord Jesus Christ."

Psalms 20, 21, and 72 no doubt refer originally
to the earthly kingdom of David and of Solomon.
Psalm 20 asks for the victory of the Messianic
king over his enemies and for the acceptance of
his sacrifices by God; Psalm 21 gives thanks for
the victory and the crowning of the king; Psalm
72 asks for justice and help for the poor, for
peace, stable government, eternal honor in the
province of the king. We pray in this Psalm for
the victory of Jesus Christ in the world, we give
thanks for the victory already won, and ask for
the establishment of the kingdom of righteousness and of peace under the king Jesus Christ.
To this theme belong also Psalm 61:7 f. and
Psalm 63:11.

The much-disputed Psalm 45 speaks of love to
the Messianic king, of his beauty, his richness, his
power. Upon marriage to this king the bride is
said to forget her people and her father's house
(v. 10) and to pay homage to the king. For him
alone she is said to adorn herself and to be led
to him with joy. That is the song and prayer of
the love between Jesus, the king, and his church
which belongs to him.

The Church

Psalms 27, 42, 46, 48, 63, 81, 84, 87, and others sing of Jerusalem, the City of God, of the great festivals of the people of God, of the temple and the beautiful worship services. It is the presence of the God of salvation in his congregation for which we here give thanks, about which we here rejoice, for which we long. What Mount Zion and the temple were for the Israelites the church of God throughout the world is for us — the church where God always dwells with his people in word and sacrament. This church will withstand all enemies (Psalm 46), its imprisonment

under the powers of the godless world will come
to an end (Psalms 126 and 137). The present
and gracious God, who is in Christ who in turn
is in his congregation, is the fulfillment of all
thanksgiving, all joy, and all longing in the
Psalms. As Jesus, in whom God himself dwells,
longed for fellowship with God because he had
become a man as we (Luke 2:49), so he prays
with us for the total nearness and presence of
God with those who are his.

God has promised to be present in the worship
of the congregation. Thus the congregation con-
ducts its worship according to God's order. But
Jesus Christ himself has offered the perfect worship by perfecting every prescribed sacrifice in
his own voluntary and sinless sacrifice. Christ
brought in himself the sacrifice of God for us
and our sacrifice for God. For us there remains
only the sacrifice of praise and thanksgiving in
prayers, hymns, and in a life lived according to
God's commands (Psalms 15 and 50). So our entire life becomes worship, the offering of thanksgiving. God wants to acknowledge such thanks-

giving and to show his salvation to the grateful (Psalms 50 and 23). To become thankful to God for the sake of Christ and to praise him in the congregation with heart, mouth, and hands, is what the Psalms wish to teach us.

Life

Many earnest Christians are struck as they pray the Psalms by how often the petition for life and good fortune occurs. From a glance at the cross of Christ there comes to many the unhealthy thought that life and the visible, earthly blessings of God are in themselves at least a questionable good, and in any case a good not to be desired. They take, then, the corresponding prayers of the Psalter to be an incomplete first stage of Old Testament piety, which is overcome in the New Testament. But in doing so they want to be more spiritual than God himself.

As the petition for daily bread includes the entire sphere of the necessities of physical life, so the petition for life, health, and visible evidences of the friendliness of God belong necessarily to the prayer which points to the God who is the creator and sustainer of this life. Bodily life is not disdainful. Precisely for its sake God has given us his fellowship in Jesus Christ, so that we can live by him in this life and then also, of course, in the life to come. For this reason he gives us earthly prayers, so that we can better recognize him, praise him, and love him. God wants the devout to prosper on earth (Psalm 37). And this desire is not set aside by the cross of Christ, but is all the more established by it. Precisely at the point where men must make many sacrifices in following Jesus, as did the disciples, they will answer, "Nothing!" to the question of Jesus, "Did you lack anything?" (Luke 22:35). The presupposition for this is the insight of the Psalms: "Better is the little that the righteous has than the abundance of many wicked" (Psalm 37:16).

Therefore we need not have a bad conscience when we pray with the Psalter for life, health, peace, and earthly goods if we only recognize, as do the Psalms themselves, that all of this is evidence of the gracious fellowship of God with us, and we thereby hold fast to the fact that God's gifts are better than life (Psalm 63:3 f.; 73:25 f.).

Psalm 103 teaches us to understand the entire fullness of the gifts of God, from the preservation of life to the forgiveness of sins, as a great unity and to come before God thanking and praising him for them (cf. also Psalm 65). The Creator gives us life and sustains it for the sake of Jesus Christ. Thus he wants to make us ready, at last through the loss of all earthly goods in death, to receive eternal life. Only for the sake of Jesus Christ and at his bidding may we pray concerning the goods of life, and for his sake we ought to do it also with confidence. But if we receive what we need, then we ought not to cease thanking God from the heart that he is so friendly to us for the sake of Jesus Christ.

Suffering

"Where do you find more miserable, more wretched, more depressing words than in the Psalms of lamentation? There you see into the heart of all the saints as into death, even as into hell. How sad and dark it is there in every wretched corner of the wrath of God" (Luther).

The Psalter gives us ample instruction in how to come before God in a proper way, bearing the frequent suffering which this world brings upon us. Serious illness and severe loneliness before God and men, threat, persecution, imprisonment, and whatever conceivable peril there is on earth are known by the Psalms (13, 31, 35, 41, 44, 54, 55, 56, 61, 74, 79, 86, 88, 102, 105, and others).

They do not deny it or try to deceive us about it with pious words. They allow it to stand as a severe attack on the faith. Occasionally they no longer focus on suffering (Psalm 88), but they all complain to God. No individual can repeat the lamentation Psalms out of his own experience; it is the distress of the entire Christian community at all times, as only Jesus Christ has experienced it entirely alone, which is here unfolded. Because it happens with God's will, indeed because God knows it completely and knows it better than we ourselves, only God himself can help. But therefore also must all our questions again and again assault God himself.

There is in the Psalms no quick and easy resignation to suffering. There is always struggle, anxiety, doubt. God's righteousness which allows the pious to be met by misfortune but the godless to escape free, even God's good and gracious will, is undermined (Psalm 44:24). His behavior is too difficult to grasp. But even in the deepest hopelessness God alone remains the one addressed. Neither is help expected from men, nor does the distressed one in self-pity lose sight of the origin and the goal of all distress, namely God. He sets out to do battle against God for God. The wrathful God is confronted countless times with his promise, his previous blessings, the honor of his name among men.

If I am guilty, why does God not forgive me? If I am not guilty, why does he not bring my misery to an end and thus demonstrate my innocence to my enemies? (Psalms 38, 44, 79). There are no theoretical answers in the Psalms to all these questions, as there are none in the New Testament. The only real answer is Jesus Christ. But this answer is already sought in the Psalms. It is common to all of them that they cast every difficulty and agony on God: "We can no longer bear it, take it from us and bear it yourself, you alone can handle suffering." That is the goal of all of the lamentation Psalms. They pray concerning the one who took upon himself our diseases and bore our infirmities, Jesus Christ. They proclaim Jesus Christ to be the only help in suffering, for in him God is with us.

The lamentation Psalms have to do with that complete fellowship with God which is justification and love. But not only is Jesus Christ the goal of our prayer; he himself also accompanies us in our prayer. He, who has suffered every want and has brought it before God, has prayed for our sake in God's name: "Not my will, but thine be done." For our sake he cried on the cross: "My God, my God, why hast thou forsaken me?" Now we know that there is no longer any suffering on earth in which Christ will not be with us, suffering with us and praying with us—Christ the only helper.

On this basis the great Psalms of trust develop. Trust in God without Christ is empty and without certainty; it is only another form of self-trust. But whoever knows that God has entered into our suffering in Jesus Christ himself may say with great confidence: "Thou art with me; thy rod and thy staff, they comfort me" (Psalms 23, 37, 63, 73, 91, 121).

Guilt

More seldom than we expect, the prayer for the forgiveness of sins meets us in the Psalms. Most Psalms presuppose complete assurance of the forgiveness of sins. That may surprise us. But even in the New Testament the same thing is true. It is an abbreviation and an endangering of Christian prayer if it revolves exclusively around the forgiveness of sins. There is such a thing as the confident leaving behind of sin for the sake of Jesus Christ.

Yet in no way does the Psalter omit the prayer of repentance. The seven so-called repentance Psalms (6, 32, 38, 51, 102, 130, 143), but not only they (also Psalms 14, 15, 25, 31, 39, 40,

41, and others) lead us into the total depth of the recognition of sin before God. They lead us to the confession of guilt and direct our complete confidence to the forgiving grace of God, so that Luther has quite correctly called them the "Pauline Psalms." Usually a special occasion leads to such a prayer. It is serious guilt (Psalms 32 and 51) or an unexpected suffering that drives to repentance (Psalms 38 and 102). In every case all hope is fixed on free forgiveness, as it has been offered to us and promised by God in his word about Jesus Christ for all times.

The Christian will find scarcely any difficulties in the praying of these Psalms. However, the question could arise as to how one is to think about the fact that Christ also prays these Psalms with us. How can the sinless one ask for forgiveness? In no way other than he can, as the sinless one, bear the sins of the world and be made sin for us (2 Corinthians 5:21). Not for the sake of his sins, but for the sake of our sins, which he has taken upon himself and for which he suffers, does Jesus pray for the forgiveness of sins. He positions himself entirely for us. He wants to be a man before God as we are. So he prays also the most human of all prayers with us and thereby demonstrates precisely that he is the true Son of God.

It is often particularly striking and offensive to evangelical Christians that in the Psalms the innocence of devout people is spoken of at least as often as is their guilt. (cf. Psalms 5, 7, 9, 16, 17, 26, 35, 41, 44, 59, 66, 68, 69, 73, 86, and others.) Here it seems obvious that there is a vestige of the so-called Old Testament works righteousness, with which the Christian can no longer begin. Yet this outlook is completely superficial and knows nothing of the depth of the Word of God. It is clear that a man can speak of his own innocence in a self-righteous way, but do we not also realize that a man can pray the most humble confession of sin very self-righteously? Talk about one's own guilt can be just as far from the Word of God as talk about one's innocence.

But the question is not which possible motives may stand behind the prayer, but whether the

content of the prayer itself is appropriate or in-
appropriate. And here it is clear that the believ-
ing Christian certainly has to say not only something about his guilt but also something equally
important about his innocence and his justification. It is characteristic of the faith of the Christian that through God's grace and the merit of
Jesus Christ he has become entirely justified and
guiltless in God's eyes, so that "there is therefore now no condemnation for those who are in
Christ Jesus" (Romans 8:1). And it is characteristic of the prayer of the Christian to hold fast
to this innocence and justification which has
come to him, appealing to God's word and thanking for it. So not only are we permitted, but di-
rectly obligated—provided we take God's action
to us at all seriously—to pray in all humiliation
and certainty: "I was blameless before him and I
kept myself from guilt" (Psalm 18:23); "If thou
testest me thou wilt find no wickedness in me"
(Psalm 17:3). With such a prayer we stand in the
center of the New Testament, in the community
of the cross of Jesus Christ.

The assertion of innocence is particularly evi-
dent in the Psalms which have to do with the
affliction that comes from godless enemies. Here
more attention is given to the rightness of the
cause of God, which, to be sure, also gives certain "rights" to the one who clings to it. That
we are persecuted for the sake of God's cause
really sets us in the position of the "righteous"
as over against the enemies of God. Along-
side the factual innocence, which of course can
never be only factual because the grace of God always has to do with us also personally, there can
be found, then, in such a Psalm a personal confession of guilt (Psalms 41:4; 69:5). That is
again only a sign that I really do depend on the
cause of God. I can then ask, even in the same
breath: "Vindicate me, O God, and defend my
cause against an ungodly people" (Psalm 43:1).

It is thoroughly unbiblical and destructive to
think that we can never suffer innocently as
long as some error still lies hidden within us.
Neither the Old Testament nor the New is of
this opinion. If we are persecuted for the sake

of the cause of God, then we suffer innocently, and we suffer with God himself; and that we are really with God and therefore innocent will demonstrate itself precisely in this that we pray for the forgiveness of our sins.

But we are innocent not only in relation to the enemies of God but also before God himself, for he sees us now united with his cause, in which he has involved us, and he forgives us our sins. Thus all Psalms of innocence flow into the hymn:

> "Jesus, thy blood and righteousness
> My beauty are, my glorious dress;
> Midst flaming worlds, in these arrayed,
>   With joy shall I lift up my head."

The Enemies

No section of the Psalter causes us greater
difficulty today than the so-called imprecatory
psalms. With shocking frequency their thoughts
penetrate the entire Psalter (5, 7, 9, 10, 13, 16,
21, 23, 28, 31, 35, 36, 40, 41, 44, 52, 54, 55, 58, 59,
68, 69, 70, 71, 137, and others). Every attempt to
pray these psalms seems doomed to failure. They
seem to be an example of what people think of as
the religious first stage toward the New Testament. Christ on the cross prays for his enemies
and teaches us to do the same. How can we still,
with these Psalms, call for the wrath of God
against our enemies? The question is therefore:
Can the imprecatory psalms be understood as

God's word for us and as the prayer of Jesus Christ? Can we as Christians pray these psalms? Note carefully again that we do not ask about possible motives, which we can never fathom anyway, but rather about the *content* of the prayer.

The enemies referred to here are enemies of the cause of God, who lay hands on us for the sake of God. It is therefore nowhere a matter of personal conflict. Nowhere does the one who prays these psalms want to take revenge into his own hands. He calls for the wrath of God alone (cf. Romans 12:19). Therefore he must dismiss from his own mind all thought of personal revenge; he must be free from his own thirst for revenge. Otherwise, the vengeance would not be seriously commanded from God. This means that only the one who is himself innocent in relation to his enemy can leave the vengeance to God. The prayer for the vengeance of God is the prayer for the execution of his righteousness in the judgment of sin. This judgment must be made public if God is to stand by his word. It must also be promulgated among those whom it concerns. I myself, with my sin, belong under this judgment. I have no right to want to hinder this judgment. It must be fulfilled for God's sake and it has been fulfilled, certainly, in wonderful ways.

God's vengeance did not strike the sinners, but the one sinless man who stood in the sinners' place, namely God's own Son. Jesus Christ bore the wrath of God, for the execution of which the psalm prays. He stilled God's wrath toward sin and prayed in the hour of the execution of the divine judgment: "Father, forgive them, for they do not know what they do!" No other than he, who himself bore the wrath of God, could pray in this way. That was the end of all phony thoughts about the love of God which do not take sin seriously. God hates and redirects his enemies to the only righteous one, and this one asks forgiveness for them. Only in the cross of Jesus Christ is the love of God to be found.

Thus the imprecatory psalm leads to the cross of Jesus and to the love of God which forgives enemies. I cannot forgive the enemies of God out of my own resources. Only the crucified Christ can do that, and I through him. Thus the carrying out of vengeance becomes grace for all men in Jesus Christ.

Certainly it is important to distinguish in relation to these psalms whether I stand in the time of promise or in the time of fulfillment, but this distinction is true for all psalms. I pray the imprecatory psalms in the certainty of their marvelous fulfillment. I leave the vengeance to God and ask him to execute his righteousness to all his enemies, knowing that God has remained true to himself and has himself secured justice in his wrathful judgment on the cross, and that this wrath has become grace and joy for us. Jesus Christ himself requests the execution of the wrath of God on his body, and thus he leads me back daily to the gravity and the grace of his cross for me and all enemies of God.

Even today I can believe the love of God and forgive my enemies only by going back to the cross of Christ, to the carrying out of the wrath of God. The cross of Jesus is valid for all men. Whoever opposes him, whoever corrupts the word of the cross of Jesus on which God's wrath must be executed, must bear the curse of God some time or another. The New Testament speaks with great clarity concerning this and does not distinguish itself at all in this respect from the Old Testament, but it also speaks of the joy of the church in that day on which God will execute his final judgment (Galatians 1:8 f.; 1 Corinthians 16:22; Revelation 18; 19; 20:11). In this way the crucified Jesus teaches us to pray the imprecatory psalms correctly.

The End

The hope of Christians is directed to the return of Jesus and the resurrection of the dead. In the Psalter this hope is not expressed literally. That which since the resurrection of Jesus has divided itself in the church into a long line of events of holy history toward the end of all things is, from the viewpoint of the Old Testament, still a single indivisible unity. Life in fellowship with the God of revelation, the final victory of God in the world, and the setting up of the messianic kingdom are objects of prayer in the psalms.

The Old Testament is not different from the New in this respect. To be sure, the psalms request fellowship with God in earthly life, but they know that this fellowship is not completed in earthly life but continues beyond it, even stands in opposition to it (Psalm 17:14 f.). So life in fellowship with God is always already on the other side of death. Death is, to be sure, the irrevocable bitter end for body and soul. It is the wages of sin, and the remembrance of it is necessary (Psalms 39 and 90. On the other side of death, however, is the eternal God (Psalms 90 and 102). Therefore not death but life will triumph in the power of God (Psalms 16:19 ff.; 49:15; 56:13; 73:24; 118:15 ff.). We find this life in the resurrection of Jesus Christ and we ask for it in this life and in that to come.

The psalms of the final victory of God and of his Messiah (2, 96, 97, 98, 110, 148-150) lead us in praise, thanksgiving, and petition to the end of all things, when all the world will give God the honor, when the redeemed people of God will reign with him eternally, when the powers of evil will fall and God alone will rule.

Petition
for the Spirit of Life

We have taken this short stroll through the Psalter in order to learn to pray a few psalms a bit better. It would not be difficult to arrange according to the Lord's Prayer all the psalms mentioned. We should have to change only slightly our arrangement of the order of the chapters. But this alone is important, that we begin to pray the psalms with confidence and love in the name of our Lord Jesus Christ.

"Our dear Lord, who has given to us and taught us to pray the Psalter and the Lord's Prayer, grants to us also the spirit of prayer and of grace so that we pray with enthusiasm and earnest faith, properly and without ceasing, for we need to do this; he has asked for it and therefore wants to have it from us. To him be praise, honor, and thanksgiving. Amen" (Luther).

The Blessing
of Morning Prayer

The entire day receives order and discipline when it acquires unity. This unity must be sought and found in morning prayer. It is confirmed in work. The morning prayer determines the day. Squandered time of which we are ashamed, temptations to which we succumb, weaknesses and lack of courage in work, disorganization and lack of discipline in our thoughts and in our conversation with other men, all have their origin most often in the neglect of morning prayer.

Order and distribution of our time become more firm where they originate in prayer. Temptations which accompany the working day will

be conquered on the basis of the morning break-
through to God. Decisions, demanded by work,
become easier and simpler where they are made
not in the fear of men but only in the sight of
God. "Whatever your task, work heartily, as serv-
ing the Lord and not men" (Colossians 3:23).
Even mechanical work is done in a more patient
way if it arises from the recognition of God and
his command. The powers to work take hold,
therefore, at the place where we have prayed to
God. He wants to give us today the power which
we need for our work.

DIETRICH BONHOEFFER:
A BIOGRAPHICAL SKETCH

by Eberhard Bethge

Dietrich Bonhoeffer's father was an eminent physician in Berlin, a psychiatrist in the first professorial chair of psychiatry in Germany; his forefathers were mayors and pastors. In the church yard in Schwäbisch-Hall there are high old gravestones bearing the name Bonhoeffer. His mother was a granddaughter of Karl von Hase, who had a great following as professor of church history in the University of Jena. As a youth, von Hase was once confined in prison because he stood up for the freedom of the student associations.

Bonhoeffer praised his mother for her natural inclination to be helpful and her quiet power to act, his father for his uncommonly clever foresight and his concentration on the possible. Among his first conscious impressions of the personality of his father was the tendency to "turn from the phraseological to the real." His training for achievement was impeccable and he was impatient toward all excessive display of emotion. "I have discovered that one of the strongest intellectual factors in the rearing of our family was that we had to surmount so many restraints with regard to factuality, clarity, naturalness, tact, simplicity, before we could express ourselves," Dietrich writes in one of his last remaining letters.

Born in Breslau on February 4, 1906, he grew up in a large family in Berlin-Grünewald. He was a strong and agile youth and did not enjoy losing in an athletic contest. And he did not lose. When he once came home with a huge victory wreath around his shoulders, he could scarcely recover from the fact that his brothers and sisters laughed at him. They thought it quite fine to win, but less fine to display it. Neighborhood

friends included the children of Adolph von Harnack and of Hans Delbrück. They celebrated
holidays together and shared musical evenings—
Dietrich became an enthusiastic pianist — had
lively discussions and went on hikes.

"In my reverie I live a great deal in nature,
specifically in the woodland glades near Fried-
richsbrunn or on the slopes from which one can
look beyond Treseburg over to the Brocken. I
lie then on my back in the grass, watch the
clouds move in the breeze, and listen to the rus-
tle of the forest. It is remarkable how strong impressions of childhood like this affect the whole
man so that it is impossible, and seems to be con-
tradictory to my nature, that we could have had
a house in the high mountains or near the sea!
The hills are for me the nature which belongs to
me and has formed me, the hills of central Germany, the Harz mountains, the Thuringian forest, the Weserberge." Thus he relived this period
while he was in prison.

In a fragment of a novel he planned to write,
he pictures the growing together of two middle-

class families into a variety of public responsibilities. A rich past is constantly renewed; there is calm but alert participation in everything human. That is the heritage for which Bonhoeffer himself was thankful. He lived to see that even in the midst of the decay of so many human relationships during the Nazi years, the large and beloved family stood together all the more closely and profoundly, even as the occupations and life goals grew diverse. No shadow fell on their common effort during the most severe tests of separation. Everyone knew that the heart of the other reacted as his own, whether in the family home or in distant and painful exile.

At the age of sixteen he knew that he wanted to study theology. After one year at the University of Tübingen, he enrolled at Berlin in 1924 and stayed there the remainder of his study time. Mornings he rode the streetcar to the university, together with the venerable Adolph von Harnack. Harnack had once been involved in lively controversy, when he wanted to alter the church's confession of faith because he wished

to say only that which he himself understood.
Now he was happy to speak with the young theo-
logian in whom he perceived a new generation
which was no longer obliged to argue about
sentences but to confess its statements of faith
while facing danger. "I have the greatest confidence that your work and your progress are on
the right track," he wrote to Dietrich when he
had to leave the Harnack study group. Bonhoeffer had heard, in addition to Harnack, the influ-
ential Berlin professors Karl Holl and Reinhold
Seeberg, Hans Lietzmann and Wilhelm Lütgert,
and had earned their respect. Nevertheless he
soon became a chief participant and promoter of
the modern "Theology of the Church," the theology of Karl Barth, with whom he had never
studied.

The story is told that he once participated in
1931 as a guest in Barth's seminar in Bonn and
threw into the discussion a citation from Luther:
"The curse of the godless can sound more pleas-
ing in the ears of God than the hallelujahs of
the pious." "Who said that?" Barth asked enthu-

siastically—and so he came to know Dietrich Bonhoeffer. At the age of twenty-one Bonhoeffer submitted his doctoral dissertation, a dogmatic investigation of *The Communion of Saints.* And in *Act and Being,* his subsequent inaugural dissertation, he ascertained with superior mastery of philosophical tools the place and significance of dialectical theology.

In 1928 he became a vicar in Barcelona. In a very skillful way he related the fascinating ritual of the bull fight. How often he sought to persuade us that there was scarcely a more aristocratic manifestation of an old culture.

After his inauguration into the faculty of theology, the church officials sent him for a year of study at Union Theological Seminary in New York, "notorious for and honored as the refuge of criticism in America, . . . a place of free expression of everything with everyone, which is made possible through the civil courage characteristic of the American and through the lack of all inhibiting officiousness in personal conversation" (Bonhoeffer, cf. report from 1931). At this time began the friendship with the two Niebuhrs. The encounter with the spirituals and the struggle of the Blacks for equal rights captivated his attention.

A few years later, while the walls rose high around Germany, he introduced his students to this world with its strange assumptions; they sang "Swing low, sweet chariot" twenty years before the radio and the concert hall made it popular. When Bonhoeffer visited America a second time, in 1939, he could no longer publish his report anywhere. He described clearly the profound possibilities which the conversation between the "Protestantism without Reformation" (U.S.A.) and the Church of the Reformation (Germany) has revealed.

Upon returning to Berlin, he lectured at the University and a circle of students immediately began to form around him. Out of the Hegel seminar came a little circle of friends. The sharp critique of the concept of the church flowed surprisingly into the admonition to love the "visible church," namely the Church of the Old

Prussian Union. Out of these lectures originated his first book to reach a popular audience: *Creation and Fall,* a theological exposition of Genesis 1-3. In addition to teaching, he served as student pastor at the technical college in Charlottenburg. The worship service, when Bonhoeffer preached, was well attended and there were crowds at the lecture series, but there was no sustained student congregation. The time was not ripe. So he gave this assignment back to the church office. He did not wish to work as a parade horse.

In 1931-32 he also took over in Berlin-Wedding a confirmation class which no one could handle. He succeeded in arousing the interest of the youngsters in the subject matter to such a degree that, many years afterwards, a group of them spent the vacation period in the cabin in Biesenthal near Berlin which Bonhoeffer had rented for them. "What blame can be placed on those whom one has thrust into life without giving them ground under their feet? Can you pass them by?" asks the proletariat of the middle-

class son in the drama fragment in which Bonhoeffer, in 1943, took up again in prison what
had at that time impressed him about these
youth who live with no restrictions. "Yes, ground
under the feet. . . . I would otherwise not have
been aware of it."

Then came the year 1933. In February a lecture of Bonhoeffer's went out over Berlin radio.
He criticized the longing for a leader who would
become a false leader if he did not clearly refuse
to become an idol and a false god to those whom
he led—an idol instead of rendering himself
superfluous by leading to the true authorities
of the father, the teacher, the judge. The broad-
cast was cut off before he finished the lecture.
As it now became clear that idol and false god
were gaining the upper hand, he accepted, in
October of 1933, the call to two German congre-
gations in London. He wanted no place in the
"German Christian"[1] establishment. "Now it is

---

[1] Translator's note: "German Christian" was the designation chosen by those church people who saw in Hitler
and the Nazi program a sign of hope for Germany and
the German church.

necessary to hold out quietly, and to ignite the
firebrand of truth in all corners of the pompous
organization, so that one day the entire struc-
ture will crumble." With that he departed from
his students.

Outside Germany he became one of the most
important interpreters of events in the German
church. Now began the deep friendship with
the Bishop of Chichester. On his trip to the
destroyed Berlin of 1945, the bishop visited
Dietrich's parents before seeing anyone else. At
the dramatic 1934 conference in Fanö, Bonhoeffer led the German youth delegation. There
arose a conflict with the delegates of the "German Christian" authorities, and Danish Bishop
Ammundsen raised his voice for the "Confessing
Church." [2] "With the conference in Fanö the
ecumenical movement has entered a new epoch,"
was his judgment in an essay entitled "The Con-

---

[2] Translator's note: "Confessing Church" was the designation chosen by those church people who saw in Hitler
and the Nazi program a threat of such proportions that
they said the church was forced into a "state of confession" in which the only real options were "yes" or "no."

fessing Church and the Ecumenical Movement"
—an epoch leading either to courteous unity
or to decisions for and against the church of
Christ.

While he prepared for a trip to Gandhi
through C. F. Andrews, the English friend of
India—the English world had awakened his interest in pacifist movements—the call came from
the Confessing Church to take over the instruction of young pastors in the seminary in Pomerania. He accepted. So in April, 1935, he moved,
with 25 vicars, to Zingst and then to Finkenwalde, living with the brothers in very makeshift
quarters. He shared with them his personal be-
longings—material as well as spiritual—his time,
and his plans. He was magnanimous, and petti-
ness disappeared as snow in the sun when one
was with him. To be sure, many students were at
first startled by the strength and power of his
thought but soon discovered that no one was
able to listen to them so well and so completely,
in order to be able to advise them and to make
demands on them which none previously had

been able to make with success. Here in the seminary everything was done in a fresh way and as for the first time—the theological work, the human life together, the taking of political positions. There were times when he became aware of how strong his influence was, and these times became the most severe testing of his faith, times when he was seized with horror at the fact that his health and his vitality, his superiority and his judgment prevailed. He hated lack of independence, and therefore he was careful to place men on their own feet.

During this period arose the war writings against all softening of doctrine: "We can no longer go behind Barmen and Dahlem,[3] because we can no longer withdraw from God's word." A controversy arose because he chose to bring together the question of the "Confessing Church" and the question of salvation. During this period he wrote *The Cost of Discipleship* (1937), in

––––––

[3] Translator's note: Barmen and Dahlem were two places in which the Confessing Church had held important meetings.

which he raised the cry against "cheap grace,"
and *Life Together* (1939), in which biblical insight was woven together with the Finkenwalde
experiences. These were the two books which,
during his lifetime, made his name most widely
known—and his summons to what it means to
be with Christ. He reawakened in many a love
for the Scriptures. Soon after this little book on
the Psalms appeared, the Nazis prohibited him
from further publishing and dissolved the seminary at Finkenwalde.

In the meanwhile other developments had begun to permeate Bonhoeffer's life and thought.
Through Hans von Dohnanyi, his brother-in-
law, he had an insight into the background of
the circle around General Fritsch and the beginning of the plans for revolution among the asso-
ciates of General Beck. At one time he had made
himself an advocate of pacifist concerns, something unheard of in Germany at the time. Now
he felt that it would be for him an illegitimate
escape from responsibility if he were to avoid
the growing contacts with the political and mili-

tary resistance movement. Not that everyone
ought to act as he did, but in his position he saw
no possibility of escape any longer into sinless-
ness and innocence. The sins of the bourgeoisie
became clear in the flight from responsibility.
This guilt he saw descending on himself and he
took his stand. Not to defend the church with
the instruments of power (that was precisely his
great disappointment, that even the "Confessing
Church" lost much of its strength because it no
longer gave its life for the Jews, but instead
fought for finances and official recognition by
the Nazi government), but to finally take up his
bourgeois responsibility as a German, he went
to the spot where God had placed him through
birth and talents. He never considered rejecting
his position in life.

On a lecture tour to America in 1939 he was
besieged by good friends with attractive invita-
tions to remain there. His ecumenical spirit and
his gift of empathy directed him to stay. But he
took one of the last ships in order to return to
obvious destruction. In his diary we read: "I do

not understand why I am here. . . . The short
prayer in which we remember our German brothers has almost overcome me. . . . If the situation
now becomes tense, I shall certainly return to
Germany. . . . I do not want to be here when
the war begins . . . . " And a few days later he
wrote: "Since I got on the ship, all inner turmoil
concerning the future has ceased." Years after
that he wrote from prison: "You must know that
I still have never regretted for a moment my return in 1939, nor anything which then followed.
It all happened in full daylight and with good
conscience. The fact that I sit here now I reckon
also as participation in the fate of Germany, to
which I committed myself."

And now began the life divided between the
duties of the Confessing Church and the tasks
of the resistance work, the visitations and the
theological work on the planned *Ethics,* which
appeared posthumously and in fragments (1949),
but which he thought of as his special task in
life. He also took a number of trips during this
period. The most difficult and exciting was the

one to Stockholm in 1942, to meet the surprised Bishop of Chichester and to inform him about which groups and names backed the eventual overthrow of the Nazi government. On the one hand, the church work under the obstacles raised by the government and during the prohibition against lectures, publication and visits to Berlin; on the other hand, the espionage passports and courier permits which were usually available only to the privileged. There were wonderful experiences of help and trust. Entire chapters of the *Ethics* were written in the guest room of the Benedictine Abbey at Ettal, others at the summer estate of Frau von Kleist in Klein-Krössin in Pomerania.

But one day it was all over. On a bright Monday in April, 1943, telephone calls informed us that Hans von Dohnanyi had been arrested in his office. Dietrich's room could still be arranged in such a way that it would lead to harmless clues. Then the expected automobile arrived. From April 5, 1943, until October 8, 1944, Bonhoeffer was in the military prison in Berlin-

Tegel. The guards soon noticed that a pastor was with them whose words were authentic and helpful. They secretly brought him into other cells to minister to despairing prisoners. They preserved his work, his articles and poems, for the future. They set up a whole courier service for his family and friends.

He lived through the prison period with great sensitivity, the seasons, the obliteration bombings, the tension of the interrogations, but to those outside he wrote: "Enjoy whatever comes your way." He thought about grace, about participating in the suffering of Christ who was "there for others," and conversed with those outside about the wonderful passion for this world which was so characteristic of the nineteenth century. He was a pastor among prisoners, and yet he did not build for himself a godly world next to the godless world. And in the massive shock of the announcement of the failure of the July 20th plot to assassinate Hitler, he placed the responsibility for public life together

with a new unbroken responsibility to bear the
results and sufferings of this involvement.

The last chapter of his life began in Septem-
ber with the discovery of the Zossen papers
(documents relating to members of the resistance movement, involving Canaris, Oster, von
Dohnanyi): Prinz-Albrecht-Strasse, Buchenwald,
Schönberg, and Flossenbürg. The contacts with
the outside world broke off. The Gestapo refused
to give any information. The last weeks Bonhoeffer spent with men and women from many
countries: Russian, English, French, Italian, and
German. Payne Best, a British officer, writes in
The Venlo Incident: "Bonhoeffer always seemed
to me to diffuse an atmosphere of happiness, of
joy in every smallest event in life, and of deep
gratitude for the mere fact that he was alive. . . .
He was one of the very few men that I have
ever met to whom his God was real and close. . . ."
They were crowded into a wood-burning bus and
driven from place to place, following the front
from uncertainty to uncertainty.

Payne Best writes: "The following day, Sun-

day, April 8, 1945, Pastor Bonhoeffer held a little
service and spoke to us in a manner which
reached the hearts of all, finding just the right
words to express the spirit of our imprisonment
and the thoughts and resolutions which it had
brought. He had hardly finished his last prayer
when the door opened and two evil-looking men
in civilian clothes came in and said: 'Prisoner
Bonhoeffer, get ready to come with us!' These
words 'Come with us' had come to mean one
thing only—the scaffold. We bade him good-bye
—he drew me aside, 'This is the end, but for me
the beginning of life.' . . . The next day at Flossenbürg, he was hanged." This happened in a
school classroom in Schönberg in the Bavarian
forest, the forest of the authors whose books he
loved so much. The Bible text for the day, on
which he had spoken, was "By his wounds we
are healed." Men of all enemy lands and of
many once hostile confessions were the brothers
who were near him at the end.

Dietrich Bonhoeffer had occasionally expressed
the thought that he would not grow old. His

generation was not permitted to allow an entire life-work to come to fruition, to bring it to a conclusion. Nevertheless, the premature breaking off of his life has given to the witness an incomparable strength. The witness of Dietrich Bonhoeffer began with the attempt to live and to say what it is to be with Christ, and it ended with teaching what it is that Christ is with us.

"It finally comes to this, if one thinks about the fragment of our life, how the whole was really planned and thought out, and of what material it consists. There are finally fragments which still belong to the rubbish heap, and there are those fragments which are meaningful only when looked at in the perspective of centuries because their fulfillment can be only a divine matter, fragments which must remain fragments. An analogy that comes to mind is the fugue. If our life also is only a slightest reflection of such a fragment, in which at least for a short while the various themes, growing ever stronger, harmonize, and in which the great counterpoint is held on to from beginning to end so that finally,

after the breaking-off point, the chorale *'Vor
deinen Thron tret ich hiermit'* can still be in-
toned, then we do not wish to complain about
our fragmentary life, but even to be glad for it"
(Letter of February 21, 1944).